My Journey

My Journey

Poetic Expressions Inspired By Faith

DeMonica D. Gladney, Esq.

Bestselling Author of *Willing to Wait*

NEW HORIZON PUBLISHERS

PEARLAND, TEXAS

MY JOURNEY: POETIC EXPRESSIONS INSPIRED BY FAITH

Unless otherwise noted, scripture references in this book are from the King James Version of the Holy Bible.

Published by:

New Horizon Publishers
8325 Broadway, Suite 202, #227
Pearland, TX 77581
Phone: (281) 436-1943
Email: info@newhorizonpublishers.com
Website: www.newhorizonpublishers.com

Cover and Interior Designed by:
Creative Publishing Book Design

ISBN: 978-0-9724229-3-2

Printed in the United States of America

This book is dedicated in loving memory to my mother, Dianne Gladney McBride, for her amazing love, life and legacy that have shaped my journey of life. She was a strong woman of faith with a big heart and inspired me to write the poem, "A Heart of Gold," in her honor. I will forever cherish our precious memories, and her legacy lives on in me.

Table of Contents

Chapter 1
Poetic Expressions on Life and Death

Chapter 2
Poetic Expressions on Faith and Patience

Chapter 3
Poetic Expressions on Unity and Freedom

Chapter 4
Poetic Expressions on Hope and Identity

Chapter 5
Poetic Expressions on Legacy and Purpose

Acknowledgements

To God for giving me a gift of faith to help me embrace the challenges of life with hope and to trust Him to do the impossible in my life. He has ordered my steps and been my source of inspiration along my journey.

To my sister, Dr. Connie Stewart, for her love, encouragement, and support that helped me get through difficult times during my journey.

To the staff of New Horizon Publishers for their hard work and commitment to this book project.

To Creative Publishing Book Design for the excellent job on my book cover and interior design.

To all of my family, friends and supporters for being a part of my journey and believing in my literary dreams.

My Journey of Life

"Wouldn't take nothing for my journey now."
—*Maya Angelou*

$\mathcal{L}$ife is a journey for all of us. It may not be a straightforward or predictable path like we expect. The road may be rough, winding and filled with many ups and downs; one day we're on the mountaintop and the next day we're in the valley. The best way for us to make the journey more meaningful is to enjoy the "good" days and learn from the "bad" days.

During my journey of life, I had to choose to walk by faith (not by sight) through the difficult times and to trust God to work all things together for my good. How we perceive our situation will depend on our level of faith. Whenever I saw my trials through the eyes of faith, God always became bigger than my problems and changed my whole perspective on life.

As a young girl, I discovered that I had a unique ability to put my inner thoughts and feelings about life on paper in a poetic form. While others were just writing in journals about their daily activities, I was using the power of my pen to write poems about real life experiences related to love, family, marriage, education, relationships, healing and death. Before I knew it, I began to write poetry on a regular basis to express my feelings about things that I was personally going through and to encourage others who were having struggles in their lives.

Over the years, my poems began to evolve beyond just general topics to what I call, "poetic expressions," to specific people in response to the problems that they shared with me. Rather than giving verbal advice, I would write them a tailor-made poem that resulted in a range of emotions, from laughter to joy and from sadness to crying. They would express surprise about what they described in my poem as "divine direction" about their specific situation. I initially didn't consider myself a poet, but I later realized that I had become sort of a "literary rapper" of rhyming lyrics without the music and a source of hope for those who read my poems. One day my maternal grandmother (a/k/a "My-My") told me that my unique style of writing poetry was a "gift" and that God was speaking through me, so that I could inspire others. At that point, I began to take my poetry writing seriously and started working on my collection of poems.

My mother had a Christian bookstore, Heavenly Treasures, back then, and I was always looking for poetry books by Christian authors to read. However, there were not a lot of poetry books available in the genre of inspirational/ Christian living. To fill that gap, I decided to publish my first poetry book, "Reflections from God: A Compilation of Inspirational Poetry". When I took that step of faith, the doors of opportunity for promoting my poetry began to suddenly swing open for me.

When I discovered that poetry books have to be marketed differently than other non-fiction books, I began to host poetry readings and book signings. I was amazed at how the words literally jumped off the page and were brought to life with my voice. Whenever I was the speaker for a conference or event (whether it was a religious, community, legal or professional organization), I started opening or closing my speech by reading a theme poem that I wrote for the occasion.

I eventually was able to recite my poems from memory, so I started calling my readings, "poetic exhortations". The word "exhortation" means an address to emphatically urge someone to do something, which was exactly what started happening when I recited my poetry. My family, friends and supporters began to share their positive feedback about my poems, such as how the poems inspired them to take a leap of faith when they were in the valley of decision or gave them hope during a difficult time in their life. This insight was the catalyst and inspiration for me to write this second poetry book, "My Journey: Poetic Expressions Inspired By Faith," which has been on hold for many years.

"My Journey" is an inspirational collection of my narrative poetry with inspiring stories about important people, places and things that have happened over time in my life and how they have impacted my journey. Inspired by my faith, each unique experience gave me the opportunity to write poetic expressions about the highs and lows of life, from birthday celebrations, anniversaries and family reunions to broken relationships, premature childbirth, and loss of a loved one. Each poem provides insight into the journey of life that we all have to go through. The poems are divided into five chapters based on the chronology of the events from my journey and the following themes: life and death, faith and patience, unity and freedom, hope and identity, and legacy and purpose.

Pack your bags and get ready to take this life-changing trip with me through "My Journey"! It's important that you focus on the journey, not the destination. You must be present in the moment during the journey and enjoy the process along the way to the final destination. That's why we are taking the scenic route on this trip, so you don't miss the small things that may turn out to be the big moments. As you navigate through the twists and turns of life reflected in my poetic expressions, you must stop to smell the roses while also dealing with the painful thorns that come along with them. While traveling on the journey, you will have an opportunity after each chapter of the book to pull over at a "rest stop" to rest, refuel and reflect on the issues that you're dealing with in your own life. After you finish reading "My Journey," I hope you will be inspired and empowered to confront the challenges in your life and to strengthen your faith as you travel through your own journey. Let the journey begin!

Chapter 1

Poetic Expressions on
Life and Death

A Miracle Child

When I heard of your early birth,
I can't describe how I felt first,
But when I laid my eyes on you,
I knew the Lord would bring you through,
I held you in the palm of my hand,
Realizing you were part of God's plan,
You were so fragile and small,
And became a blessing to us all,
Your destiny helped start your course,
And I knew God was your life source,
I watched you take each breath,
So concerned about your health,
I prayed that God would make you whole,
And save your spirit, body, and soul,
I loved you with all my heart,
And watched God do His part,
You grew stronger day by day,
The doctors did not know what to say,
Your parents were elated to take you home,
And I knew it would not be very long,

Until I realized how special you are,
There's no one like you near or far,
So it only took me a little while,
To know you are a miracle child.

♥ In Loving Memory of My Cousin ♥
Meagan Ariel James
March 5, 1995 – July 9, 2020

A Grandmother's Legacy

Faithful, trustworthy and kind,
A more virtuous woman who can find,
A humble, committed servant of the Lord,
Who stood by faith when times were hard,
She was called to do her destined part,
And gave her all with such a pure heart,
A true example of God's unconditional love,
Speaking much wisdom from heaven above,
Always very compassionate, yet also firm,
Meek but also knowing when to be stern,
She loved to preach the Lord's Word,
And with authority His voice could be heard,
Her children rose up and called her blessed,
Because she had exceeded all of the rest,
True strength and honor is what she wore,
As she walked through every open door,
Elegant and graceful with her head held high,
All one could really say was "My-My,"
She ran the race until the end of her course,
Making so many sacrifices with no remorse,
She had many tussles with the enemy,
Yet still praising God for each victory,

And her living will not be in vain,

For she desired to glorify His name,

She stored up an inheritance for us all,

When she fully answered her divine call,

We may still mourn because she is gone,

But rest assured her memory lives on,

For she has finally been made free,

And we can rejoice for she left us a legacy.

♥ In Loving Memory of My Grandmother ♥
Pastor E. M. Gladney
June 7, 1933 - November 16, 2003

We Are Family

My dear grandmother has gone on home,
And she's counting on us to carry on,
She's the glue that held this family together,
During each storm that we had to weather,
She is watching us from heaven above,
And she wants us to walk in true love,
The pain of her loss runs so very deep,
But her precious memories we must keep,
She left a spiritual legacy for us all,
So now it's up to us to answer the call,
Instead we've allowed division to come in,
And cause confusion and strife from within,
My brother and sister are not my foe,
The enemy has done this, we know,
He just wants to conquer and divide,
But this foul spirit can no longer hide,
It's time to let go of those childish things,
And recognize what family really means,
It is up to all of us to close this big gap,
And put our family back on the map,
We can't take back the words we've said,
But we can put all the foolishness to bed,

We must choose to let the past go,
And let the love between us show,
We've all been hurt and feel much pain,
But fighting each other won't bring any gain,
Let's unite together against the real enemy,
Then watch how fast he begins to flee,
His main goal is to make sure that we fail,
But the Lord has ordained us to prevail,
Surely things have been so very hard,
But we should be truly thanking God,
For He will always comfort and keep us,
If only with our whole heart will we trust,
For our many blessings, we'll start to see,
When we finally realize that we are family.

Happy Mother's Day

Mother, you are a special someone,
Your hard work is never done,
You always know just what to say,
To wipe all of my tears away,
You're full of so much joy and love,
You've always trusted in God above,
You knew God would show you what to do,
To give you strength to see us through,
You're always determined and strong,
Yet admitting you were sometimes wrong,
You have faith like a mustard seed,
Believing God would provide every need,
You have trained me up just right,
And prayed for me day and night,
You've sacrificed through every test,
So that I could have the very best,
I may not give you the praise you deserve,
But I know the important role you serve,
I know that I must honor and obey,
Because you've taught me the right way,

While I may not say it often enough,
But I thank and love you so much,
For you, mother, I will always pray,
As I honor you on this Mother's Day.

Happy Father's Day

I want to honor you on this special day,
For all the many things you do and say,
I want to thank you for just being there,
And always showing how much you care,
You encouraged me when I was sad,
And stood by me through the good and bad,
You wiped my tears when I fell down,
But still corrected me when I frowned,
You raised me up in the right way,
And always knew just what to say,
You showered me with much love,
And guided me with wisdom from above,
You taught me so much about life,
So I would never have to think twice,
You made many sacrifices for me,
And your sincere heart I could see,
You worked hard so I could have the best,
And wouldn't have to settle for anything less,
You never gave up on me no matter what,
And that's why I appreciate you so much,

I cherish all of the memories we've shared,
And I'm a better person because you cared,
You are very special in so many ways,
And I wish you a very Happy Father's Day.

My Heavenly Father

I want to honor You on this special day,
For You've touched my life in many ways,
I thank You for your unconditional love,
For sending your Word from heaven above,
You knew me in my mother's womb,
And You rose up for me from the tomb,
You predestined my life from the very start,
And then created in me a clean heart,
You have ordered my steps each day,
And You answer me whenever I pray,
You have always been so good to me,
For You delivered and set me free,
You have always supplied all my need,
And my expectations You continue to exceed,
You gave me a measure of Your faith,
And gave me strength to run the race,
You have started a good work in me,
And will continue it through eternity,
Through You was I finally made whole,
For You saved my body, spirit and soul,
All I desire to do is Your perfect will,
And for my divine destiny to be fulfilled,

I appreciate You just for who You are,
For there's no father like You near or far,
You are very special in so many ways,
And I wish you a Heavenly Father's Day.

My Spiritual Father

I want to honor you on this special day,
For all the many things you do and say,
I thank God for sending you into my life,
And for all your godly wisdom and advice,
No natural father to tell me what to do,
But you were there to see me through,
A true example of God's unconditional love,
Giving words of knowledge from above,
You were more than a mentor to me,
For you prayed until I was set free,
You walked me through spiritual things,
When the enemy tried to come on the scene,
I have had more instructors than a few,
But not many fathers that were like you,
You were such a big part of my "new" birth,
While helping me to raise my self-worth,
For you laid your anointed hands on me,
And encouraged me to become all I can be,
You also stirred up gifts that were in me,
And my true purpose could you see,
You are truly a man after God's own heart,
For it was a divine connection from the start,

You watched over my heart and soul,
And showed me how to become whole,
I followed you as you followed Christ,
And I never ever had to think twice,
For I knew you were to impart unto me,
And help me to fulfill my divine destiny,
I am grateful that you answered your call,
For you have been a blessing to us all,
Now I hope that you can finally see,
Just how much you really mean to me,
You are very special in so many ways,
So I honor you as my Spiritual Father today.

The Gift of Life

Life is fragile like a delicate flower,
For no man knows his last day or hour,
Each day has been numbered like the sand,
For there's an appointed time for every man,
Precious is every single breath that we take,
Regardless of the decisions that we make,
For we all are a part of God's divine plan,
And life and death are still in His hands,
To everything there's a time and season,
Even in death, we must see the reason,
For many pioneers have come and gone,
But now it's up to all of us to carry on,
The legacy that they have left behind,
For destiny and purpose we must find,
Our loved ones have gone on to glory,
And we're still here to tell their story,
So let's live each day like it's our last,
For this life we live will one day pass,
We still only have just one life to live,
And one opportunity to love and give,

So let your life be an example to many,
For chances to help others are plenty,
So there's no need to even think twice,
We must now embrace the gift of life.

REST STOP 1

"The only impossible journey
is the one you never begin."
—*Tony Robbins*

While traveling on a road trip, a rest stop gives you several rest and refuel options for your convenience. You can go to the restroom, grab a snack or fill your gas tank. It all depends on what your needs are at that time.

After reading the poetic expressions related to the celebration of life and death and how specific experiences impacted my journey, you must pull over at this first rest stop to refuel and reflect on what you need during this part of the journey.

REFUEL:
Take a breath to rest your mind, nourish your soul and refresh your spirit by meditating on the following scriptures:

Deuteronomy 30:19

John 10:10

2 Corinthians 5:8

Romans 14:8

Revelation 21:4

REFLECT:

Reflect on your personal thoughts, feelings and observations from this part of the journey and write them down on the following "Reflect on the Journey" page.

REFLECT ON THE JOURNEY

RESUME THE JOURNEY

We are on the road again! I enjoy waking up on a Saturday morning for a short road trip to the movies. My first stop at the theatre is to get popcorn since it's the best part of my whole experience. Likewise, you should grab your box of popcorn and get ready to watch the rest of the movie. Before we resume the journey, you should write down the lessons learned from your reflections below.

____

____

____

____

____

____

____

____

Chapter 2

Poetic Expressions on
Faith and Patience

Standing Still

You already asked the Lord what to do,
Wondering if He will see you through,
You ask, "should I run or should I walk?"
"Should I listen or should I talk?"
"Should I go or should I stop and wait?"
Then you remember that God is never late,
You realize He did not tell you to go,
So you should not move fast or slow,
Begin to seek the Lord to know His will,
Until that time, you must stand still,
Be like a tree planted by the river,
And watch the Lord begin to deliver,
For after you have done all to stand,
Just continue to stand with all you can,
For the Lord will do all of the rest,
And bring you through this ordained test,
He shall reveal His true purpose and will,
But only while you are standing still.

Get a Revelation

Do not be moved by what you feel,
But trust what God has already revealed,
Though the promise appears to tarry,
There's no need for you to get weary,
For the promise will come in due season,
So you can stop asking God for a reason.

Time to Prepare

If you take the time to prepare,
There will be no need for despair,
If in God you will only believe,
He will get you ready to receive,
The promises you are waiting for,
And the many blessings He has in store.

Just Realize

If the promise, you will just realize,
You will not have to compromise,
And end up settling for anything less,
Than what God considers His best,
For only by faith you must stand,
In order to possess your promised land.

It Will Soon Manifest

What you believe is what you get,
Although you have not seen it yet,
God has an appointed time for you,
After your preparation is through,
So don't you listen to all the rest,
For your promise will soon manifest.

Let Us Receive Our King

When the fullness of time had come,
God sent His only begotten Son,
To bring salvation to a sinful world,
And save every man, woman, boy and girl,
The long-awaited Messiah came to the earth,
To fulfill the prophecy of His virgin birth,
In Bethlehem, the Savior was born,
So His royal lineage could be sworn,
Jesus was born to be the divine King,
And the Lord and ruler over everything,
He came veiled in the form of a child,
Not in all His majesty, but meek and mild,
Since Jesus Christ was born in a manger,
His own people treated him like a stranger,
They didn't know Him as the Conquering King,
With power and authority to reign supreme,
He was destined to sit on David's throne,
And His eternal kingdom will go on and on,
The Christ Child came to be the True Light,
To turn the darkness of this world bright,
His miraculous birth was great joy for all,
But not everyone answered His call,

Even His own, they received him not,
For the promised Messiah they soon forgot,
He was mocked as "King of the Jews" at the cross,
Yet He was still able to save all of the lost,
He came into this world to answer their cry,
But they didn't realize He was born to die,
And that He rose up with all power in the end,
Or that He would even come back again,
But we'll recognize Him when He cracks the sky,
And the world will know He is the Most High,
For the next time He'll come in all His glory,
So make sure you understand the full story,
For Jesus is the only true King of kings,
And heaven and earth will rejoice and sing,
Oh joy to the world for our King is come,
Let's worship Him like it should be done,
At Christmas, let's celebrate Jesus our King,
Because He created the earth and everything,
For God gave us His most precious gift,
So our praise and worship should be swift,
For in our hearts, peace will He bring,
And now come let us receive our King.

Quench My Thirsty Soul

Lord, I need You to quench my thirsty soul,
To refresh and heal me and make me whole,
When I drink from the well, I always thirst again,
For that water doesn't satisfy my longing within,
I keep going back to the same well to draw,
Yet my healing and restoration seem so far,
All the water in this deep well cannot sustain me,
For only You have the water that can set me free,
Give me Your living water so that I thirst no more,
Let this well of water spring up in me forever more,
I thought a man could fulfill all of my inner needs,
But I have decided to Your words I must take heed,
I will put down my waterpot to receive Your well,
And of this great gift of God, to all will I tell,
You know me from the inside and the out,
Only Your living water can minister to my drought,
For once I drink of this water that only You can give,
I know I will be completely satisfied and fulfilled,
For it will totally renew my heart, mind and soul,
And only then will I be made completely whole,
The many pains of my past can I no longer hold,
When You just step in to quench my thirsty soul.

Problem Solved

There was a problem that came our way,
Neither of us knew exactly what to say,
You were hurt and so unsure,
Talking it over was the only cure,
You tried to hide behind empty words,
But your true feelings could be heard,
You had decided that we should be mad,
But instead we both were only very sad,
What they did to us was not at all right,
But they were still forgiven in my sight,
We know they made a big mistake,
But we can't give up for our own sake,
We needed to hear each other's voice,
Before we made the wrong choice,
I felt like I had lost a part of me,
Now I think you're beginning to see,
Why our problem, we must overcome,
Because we can conquer all as one,
We have never been through this before,
And our problem has taught us more,

For I have now become more close to you,
For this was a hard lesson for two,
While you learned from me and me from you,
Our problem was solved by talking it through.

It's Harvest Time

If you plant a seed and let it grow,
You will surely reap what you sow,
The harvest you will soon receive,
If you hold on to what you believe,
Even though you can't see "it" yet,
What you sow is what you will get,
For it's your time and your season,
And it's coming to pass for that reason,
So start counting down each day,
For your blessing is on the way,
When you reflect back on the wait,
You may have thought "it" was too late,
Well you better get ready for the climb,
Because now … *"It's Harvest Time"*.

REST STOP 2

"Focus on the journey not the destination."
—*Greg Anderson*

While traveling by airplane, you can get an upgrade to first class with elite status on your flight (a rest stop in the sky). First class perks include lounge access, early boarding, hot meals, free movies and coat checks. You just have to tell the flight attendant what you need at that moment.

After reading the poetic expressions about the importance of having faith and patience to receive God's promises and how they worked together to strengthen me along my journey, you must land at this second rest stop to refuel and reflect on what you need during this part of the journey.

REFUEL:

Take a breath to rest your mind, nourish your soul and refresh your spirit by meditating on the following scriptures:

Hebrews 6:12; 10:23; 10:35; 11: 1-6; 12:2

Mark 11: 22-24

Corinthians 5:7

Galatians 6:9

James 1:2-4

REFLECT:

Reflect on your personal thoughts, feelings and observations from this part of the journey and write them down on the following "Reflect on the Journey" page.

REFLECT ON THE JOURNEY

43

RESUME THE JOURNEY

Prepare for takeoff! Whenever I take an international trip for work, I go through my travel checklist before I pack my bags. I want to make sure I have everything that I need for the long journey. Likewise, you should check your bags to make sure you only packed your essentials because some things may need to be left behind. Before we resume the journey, you should write down the lessons learned from your reflections below.

____

____

____

____

____

____

____

____

____

Chapter 3

Poetic Expressions on
Unity and Freedom

The Past Fifty Years

As we celebrate the past fifty years,
Remember all the struggles and tears,
Our Black lawyers had to come together,
To help make the legal profession better,
We saw racism and injustice on every hand,
Yet our founders were willing to take a stand,
For they realized the true power of unity,
To protect the rights of our community,
A new generation of lawyers stepped in,
To build on all that our founders began,
The last ten years were a time of change,
All of our priorities we had to rearrange,
For many victories seemed to fade away,
But our determination is here to stay,
So don't think this race is over or done,
Because all we're doing is passing the baton,
While this last decade draws to an end,
There is still one message we need to send,
Since we have already honored our history,
Now it's time to further our legal legacy.

Standing on Their Shoulders

Justice and equality is why we fight,
To fix the wrongs and make them right,
We have to stand for those who can't,
And make up our minds not to faint,
Back in the day, our word was our bond,
But now we say things we have not done,
Let's not make promises we can't keep,
So that we don't let down those who weep,
Our forefathers have already paved the way,
For all of the opportunities we have today,
They boldly took a stand way back then,
Enduring many struggles, so we could win,
The economic crisis is not what it seems,
And can't stop us from fulfilling our dreams,
True change does not ever happen overnight,
So we need to keep the vision right in sight,
For we can say, "Free at last, Free at last,"
But our future is actually built on our past,
Because we have a long journey ahead of us,
And commitment and dedication is a must,
We must work hard now while it is still day,
And make sure that we mean what we say,

We definitely can't let our community down,
Nor can we just throw our integrity around,
To whom much is given, much is required,
So we can't just give up when we get tired,
Because the Lord will be our guiding light,
And strengthen and equip us all for this fight,
Since only together can we reach the top,
So let's move forward and don't dare stop,
The race is not given to the swift or strong,
But to those who are determined to go on,
True freedom and liberty are in our hands,
So we must commit to do the best we can,
For so very long, we have talked the talk,
But now it is time for us to walk the walk,
It's not enough to just say, "Yes, we can,"
For on their shoulders, we must stand.

Respect Yourself

When you look in the mirror, what do you see?
Because how you see yourself is the real key,
Do you see a stranger looking back at you?
Whose hopes and dreams you have no clue,
Whether you are light, dark, big, small,
Or even smart, average, short or tall,
Your looks don't define who you really are,
Or determine if in life you will get very far,
I hope you know that you are somebody,
So don't let anyone say you're a nobody,
Don't allow people to call you bad names,
Or make you play the old insecurity game,
Your life may be full of many ups and downs,
But start looking up when you hit the ground,
You asked, "Why don't they treat me right?
Instead of making me mad enough to fight,
Or just give me a chance to prove myself,
Not pre-judging me like everyone else,"
Well it is all about learning true respect,
So you can show them what you expect,
You teach people just how to treat you,
If you don't value "you," they're not going to,

If you want respect, you must give it away,
And be careful about the things you say,
You don't need anyone to validate you,
Just make up your mind to go through,
Refuse to be beaten, abused, or misused,
And to break the cycle you must first choose to
RESPECT YOURSELF,
By letting go of the pain from your past,
And start focusing on your future at last,
Those who were supposed to protect you,
They may have wrongly violated you too,
Even disrespected you in the worse way,
And you may have flashbacks about that day,
But you must respect your mind, body and soul,
For your true beauty is inside if the truth be told,
Don't be tempted with sex, alcohol or drugs,
Or enticed to waste your time hanging in clubs,
All the negative things they said are not true,
You are special and unique for just being you,
You do deserve to be treated like a queen,
So don't you settle for anything in between,
Tell them what they see is what they get,
A young Black sister who just won't quit,
It doesn't even matter what they say or do,
Because your decisions will depend on you,
So no more self-pity or low self-esteem,
For things are never as bad as they seem,

You still have your whole life ahead of you,
And you can become anything you want to,
Don't fret about whatever comes your way,
Because it can't change your value anyway,
Now I think you are finally beginning to see,
The power you have when you say "I like me,"
It's time to take your self-worth off the shelf,
And start now to RESPECT YOURSELF.

A Fond Farewell

It has already been six years or more,
Since I first arrived onto this floor,
It wasn't long before I saw contracts galore,
And had many clients lined up at my door,
I was so eager to learn the business of gas,
And everything began to move really fast,
Commercial agreements were on the brain,
And total immersion in the legal review game,
Issues ranging from warranty to choice of law,
Many negotiations didn't seem to get very far,
Yet we tackled tough issues to get to a "win-win,"
And we usually got our preferred terms in the end,
When legal issues arose, the lawyers got involved,
And with teamwork, we would get things resolved,
Then, it would be time for the final functional review,
But we were not done until the process was through,
And the next question would be who will sign below,
For we need a contract in place before gas can flow,
Because once the contract execution was all done,
It was time to start working on the next one,
Don't forget all the memories we've shared,
And the times when our success was declared,

Over the years, clients have come and gone,
But I'm glad to be leaving you all to carry on,
I have to say goodbye, but wish I could stay,
For you know, I am only a phone call away,
So please make sure that you do stay in touch,
And know that I will miss you all very much,
It has truly been a pleasure working with you,
For the lessons learned were more than few,
I enjoyed being on the team as you can tell,
But now it's time to wish you a fond farewell.

Celebrating Ten Years

Ten years of ministry and service is the theme,
So let me tell the story about all the in between,
When our Pastors first met was not by chance,
Or that their friendship would turn into romance,
A divine connection was started over the phone,
And their conversation seemed to go on and on,
They both held on to every word that was said,
The next thing they knew, it's was time to wed,
They were both anointed to work their text,
And would put the Word into proper context,
They would lift up the Lord every time they preach,
Not fully knowing all the people they would reach,
Building a ministry from the ground up was a lot,
But it wasn't long until God appointed their spot,
They committed to taking the gospel to the world,
To bring healing to every man, woman, boy and girl,
Along the way, many people have come and gone,
However the work of the Lord continued to go on,
As their lives began to move in a new direction,
They kept ministering for the saints' perfection,
Although the road has been very long and hard,
They both were truly dedicated to obeying God,

They were preaching while also laying hands,
And Satan didn't want this anointed duo to stand,
They wondered why things seem to be so rough,
Instead of getting easier, times seem to get tough,
The Lord was only preparing them for His very best,
Because they submitted their will and said, "Yes!"
I can't believe that ten years has passed so fast,
Until reflecting on the ups and down of their past,
They never imagined this life when they first met,
And didn't even know what God had in store yet,
The Lord had already sealed their true fate,
Because they held on and were "willing to wait,"
As this decade in their lives has come to an end,
A new season of manifestation is about to begin,
The number ten simply means a divine order,
So they no longer have to work hard, but smarter,
For this is their time and season to be blessed,
So just watch their blessings start to manifest,
They must step out by faith as their lives bloom,
For all that they've dreamed of is coming soon,
So we saluted them with much love and cheers,
As we all joyfully celebrate their ten years.

We Do It Better Together

It's time for us to refocus on the vision,
And to build on the legacy of this division,
The dreams of our founders will take place,
If we just remain strong and finish the race,
Many women trailblazers paved the way,
So that we all could be where we are today,
We've been called to help our community,
And ensure they have justice and equality,
Women lawyers need our help everywhere,
And it's up to us to show how much we care,
We are our sisters keeper is what we've said,
But then we act like that promise is dead,
We can no longer just pretend like all is well,
Or be afraid of being honest enough to tell,
Those things that have been on our heart,
So we can really have a brand new start,
We can't keep dwelling on things in the past,
But commit to make what we have now last,
It doesn't matter what's been said or done,
For we can't walk together unless we're one,
We have to embrace our present in true unity,
And then from all limitations we can be free,

The only way that we can truly move ahead,
Is to follow through with all that we've said,
While knowing our history is important too,
Our future still will depend on each of you,
So let's remember why we're in this fight,
To do our very best to make things right,
Although we've had many ups and downs,
We can learn from the mistakes we've found,
What we do should never just be about us,
When we say that in God we put our trust,
To whom much is given, much is required of us,
So our integrity and dedication is a must,
We are blessed to be a blessing to others,
With love, our many faults can be covered,
For we must always speak the truth in love,
And be led and guided by the Lord above,
For we must have respect for each other,
And be willing to listen to one another,
So I hope we are ready to turn the page,
And build on all the progress we've made,
As we begin to take a closer look at our goals,
We are now ready to see the vision unfold,
There is no "I" when we work as a team,
I hope you all understand what I mean,
For there's no storm that we can't weather,
Once we realize that we do it better together.

The Dream Is a Reality

It's time for us to celebrate "The Dream,"
And to remember what it really means,
Our ancestors had been bound in chains,
Waiting until their day of freedom came,
It was proclaimed over 145 years ago,
To free all of the slaves and let them go,
But some of the owners refused to comply,
And the forces demanded to know why,
For the news of freedom was a little late,
And a failed attempt to change their fate,
It's not just always simply black or white,
But the truth had to be brought to light,
All the slaves were eventually set free,
But they didn't leave their slave mentality,
They were beaten and broken down,
Heartache and pain is all they found,
Finally free to live the American Dream,
Life, liberty, happiness and all in between,
But injustice tried hard to hold them back,
And remind them of all that they lacked,
When they thought racism was far away,
It was apparent that it was here to stay,

Dr. Martin Luther King, Jr. came on the scene,
And began to move forward with his dream,
The struggle for justice has been a long fight,
With many obstacles to making things right,
Over 45 years later, a Black man won the race,
And in the White House, he took his place,
For change does not happen overnight,
So we need to keep the "dream" in sight,
We say that the Black man is still not free,
But our real worst enemy is called "me,"
The economic crisis is not what it seems,
And can't stop us from fulfilling our dreams,
"Free at last, Free at last," is what we sing,
But now it's really time for freedom to ring,
For only together can we reach the top,
So let's move forward and refuse to stop,
Until we all finally achieve true equality,
Can we say that "the dream is a reality"?

God's Girls Gone Wild

You better watch out if you're expecting mild,
Because God's Girls have officially gone wild,
For it's time to celebrate our true womanhood,
And how much God loved us when no one could,
We have to go back to when He first made man,
For it was not good until He created wo-man,
We were fearfully and wonderfully made,
And the apple of His eye is where we stayed,
God had fashioned His greatest creation yet,
So what they see is exactly what they get,
A woman anointed and appointed for His use,
Being about His business without any excuse,
He gave us a womb so things could be birthed,
And to help us to fulfill our purpose on this earth,
Our role as mothers is the first to come to mind,
But we wear so many hats of different kinds,
We're also wives, daughters, sisters and friends,
Our hard work and sacrifice seem to never end,
For we are always trying to hold it all together,
And still helping to make everyone else feel better,
But we have to learn how to let down our guard,
Laying aside the weights when things get hard,

We're gifted to multi-task and get things done,
To bring home and cook the bacon all in one,
We even come in all colors, shapes, and sizes,
So let's be real and take off all the disguises,
It doesn't matter if we're big, small or round,
Or yellow, vanilla, dark chocolate or brown,
We are all so beautiful just the way we are,
And in His strength, we've made it this far,
We know why our haters have so much lip,
But we are not aggressive, just equipped,
For the Word says that we can do all things,
So, just do you and raise your self-esteem,
Now we know who we were created to be,
And we're empowered to fulfill our destiny,
For God loved all of us before we even knew,
And crushed the enemy before we had a clue,
So we can rejoice for we're one of "God's Girls,"
And a force to be reckoned with in this world,
So from day one, our God was wild about us,
And being wildly in love with Him is a must,
So we have a reason to strut our stuff in style,
And that's why "God's Girls" have gone wild.

I'm Every Woman

If you really want to know who I am,
And why people refer to me as "ma'am,"
For I am fearfully and wonderfully made,
And dressed to the tee with my hair laid,
I light up the room whenever I walk in,
Not just fitting in, but setting the trend,
I may look good from my head to my toe,
But there are many things you don't know,
For I carry the many burdens of this world,
And still hear the cries from my inner girl,
I have had to be all things to everyone,
And all my work seems to never be done,
I have volunteered to help with this and that,
However, I can't keep up with my many hats,
First of all, don't forget that I am a woman,
But I am still expected to think like a man,
I'm a mother, wife, daughter and sister too,
And a lawyer and counselor to name a few,
I'm trying so hard to keep it all together,
Hoping that one day it will get better,
So busy taking care of everyone else,
Sometimes, I end up neglecting myself,

But remember, I have needs just like you,
I want to be nurtured and pampered too,
I realize that my sacrifices are not in vain,
But it's time for me to master this game,
So now I'm bringing in every part of me,
Taking off my mask, so everyone can see,
So I can focus on my mind, body and soul,
For I truly want to be completely whole,
I will let the Lord be my guiding light,
For I know I'm not alone in this fight,
My gifts and talents you may not see,
But look closer because "it's" all in me,
I can finally walk into my full destiny,
For I have just discovered the real me,
I hold my head high and lift my hand,
Because now I know, I'm EVERY woman.

REST STOP 3

"The journey not the arrival matters."
—*T.S. Eliot*

While traveling on a cruise ship, your vacation can become a makeshift rest stop on water. After the ship sets sail, you can relax by the pool, hit the gym or enjoy the food buffets. Your activities will depend on what your needs are at that time.

After reading the poetic expressions about balancing individual freedom with corporate unity, you must disembark at this third rest stop to refuel and reflect on what you need during this part of the journey.

REFUEL:

Take a breath to rest your mind, nourish your soul and refresh your spirit by meditating on the following scriptures:

Psalm 133: 1

John 8:32, 36

Romans 8:1-2

Galatians 5:1

Ephesians 4:3, 13

REFLECT:

Reflect on your personal thoughts, feelings and observations from this part of the journey and write them down on the following "Reflect on the Journey" page.

REFLECT ON THE JOURNEY

68

RESUME THE JOURNEY

All aboard! I have only taken two cruises in my lifetime. I don't like feeling stuck onboard a ship in the middle of the ocean, so I realized that a cruise does not meet my vacation needs. You should check your travel list to confirm if there is anything that does not fit your journey, so you can scratch it off. Before we resume the journey, you should write down the lessons learned from your reflections below.

____

____

____

____

____

____

____

____

____

Chapter 4

Poetic Expressions on
Hope and Identity

Your First Birthday

Now that you have turned one,
Your life has only really just begun,
You were so precious from your birth,
And have a divine purpose on this earth,
Your parents shower you with much love,
For you are truly a gift from heaven above,
As you start to experience this big world,
Know that you'll always be a special girl,
I pray that your purpose will be fulfilled,
And that you will always seek God's will,
For the future holds so much for you,
And you will be blessed in all that you do,
As you grow up from now until then,
Never forget the beauty you have within,
I am so honored on this special day,
To wish you a happy first birthday!

Stolen Identity

I did not know my identity was at risk,
While I was going through life in total bliss,
All of a sudden my ID was just stolen away,
But I couldn't narrow it down to a specific day,
Well, it could have been when I failed my test,
Or when I was told to be better than the rest,
Sometime between my childhood and now,
I had lost myself, but didn't fully know how,
From the outside, everything looked fine,
But the face I saw in the mirror wasn't mine,
I began a long journey in search of me,
Yet who I really was, I could no longer see,
I had somehow lost sight of the "real" me,
Blinded by my past and filled with insecurity,
I was not sure about my true self-worth,
Or for what purpose I was put on this earth,
Like everyone else, I wanted to be affirmed,
But I was taken advantage of at every turn,
I had been robbed by bad relationships,
And those who loved only with their lips,
The enemy wanted me to feel ashamed,
And to focus on someone else to blame,

So I started to really question who I am,
While feeling pressured and overwhelmed,
My good name was secretly taken from me,
And it left me as devastated as can be,
But it didn't compare to what came next,
When I couldn't put my life into context,
All of the missing pieces that I lacked,
I had to take steps to get them all back,
But I didn't want to remember the past,
Yet I wasn't ready to take off my mask,
I had lost all my confidence and worth,
And just couldn't let go of all the hurt;
A head-on collision tried to take me out,
Bringing even more fear and self-doubt,
For I was living my life for everyone else,
And not having any quality time for myself,
I was driven to succeed by all that was said,
And did whatever was needed to get ahead,
A real perfectionist through and through,
My self-esteem became tied to what I do,
How it all happened, I did not have a clue,
And the trials I went through were not few,
But I knew that I was a threat to the enemy,
That's why he didn't want me to know "me,"
I had been struggling to find the right way,
And always worried about what people say,

Yet God knew me in my mother's womb,
So my God-given identity I could assume,
Now that I know what He said about me,
From others' opinions I am finally free,
I had to fight to get my true identity back,
And follow the Truth instead of the facts,
The enemy came to steal, kill and destroy,
But when Jesus came, he didn't get very far,
So now I can start living the abundant life,
For I know that my "real" identity is in Christ,
And I finally know who I was created to be,
But first I had to reclaim my stolen identity.

Identify What Is Missing

I have to identify what is missing,
So to get started I had to go fishing,
Searching through the pieces of my life,
That's when I was forced to look twice,
To figure out what happened to "me,"
So I could recover my stolen identity.

Inventory the Actual Loss

My identity had already been taken,
But I didn't know until I was awakened,
I had to do an inventory of all of my loss,
Then I started counting up all the costs,
While I kept searching to find the real me,
And confirm the true source of my identity.

Inspect All the Findings

You have to inspect all of your findings,
And look closer when your life is unwinding,
You need to check out all of your sources,
And recognize the invisible stealing forces,
All of your pockets still need to be checked,
If you haven't found all that's missing yet.

Initiate the Full Recovery

You have to initiate your full recovery,
Now that you've done your self-discovery,
All that was missing you should finally see,
So snatch it all back from the "real" enemy,
For only then will you be completely free,
To rightfully reclaim your stolen identity.

Walk Into Your Destiny

As you celebrate the past twenty-two years,
We want to salute you with love and cheers,
But let's first take a trip down memory lane,
So everyone knows from where you came,
With just a vision to reach the "total man,"
You entrusted the ministry into God's hand,
In the carpenter's building you got your start,
And your family and friends became a part,
You ministered to the spirit, body and soul,
Praying that your flock would become whole,
What God spoke to you, He began to prove,
So you stepped out by faith and made a move,
To a new place where your roots were planted,
And the desires of your heart were granted,
Preaching and teaching the Word to the lost,
Giving your whole heart regardless of the cost,
Then the time came when you passed the baton,
But you knew then that your work was not done,
When you began to answer your destined call,
The enemy tried hard to make your ministry fall,
Over the years many people had come and gone,
And many days you felt like you were all alone,

But you had to go back to what God said first,
And then our church experienced a "new" birth,
You questioned where you would go from here,
Yet you embraced the "new" vision with no fear,
We know it has been a long and challenging ride,
But you have finally made it to the other side,
For your divine vision has stood the test of time,
And many blessings is what you will soon find,
As you go to that next level in your ministry,
And begin to fully walk into your destiny.

Life in Bloom

You ask how to live your "life in bloom,"
So full that you don't have enough room,
For the blessings that are coming your way,
And you're living life to the fullest each day,
When you're operating at your highest peak,
And fulfilling your purpose is all you seek,
Once you're not afraid to dream again,
Only then does your life really begin,
God gave you the power to get wealth,
So you can prosper and be in good health,
Because you only have one life to live,
What you get depends on how you give,
And you shall know a tree by its fruit,
So it's time for you to spread your roots,
But first be sure that you plant your seed,
Then give it all of the water that it needs,
And from underground it can break free,
Into the beautiful flower it was meant to be,
Just watch the delicate bud begin to grow,
As a sign that you will reap what you sow,
So once each petal begins to open wide,
You can see all the beauty that's inside,

But only after the flower blossoms in full,
And the rays of sunshine it starts to pull,
Your life can also flourish like that rose,
If you open the areas that were closed,
The Master Orchestrator is still in control,
So you can stop putting your life on hold,
And step out by faith on what God said,
So the world can see your flower bed,
No longer can you just simply exist,
Or allow your vision to only be a wish,
Now it's your season and harvest time,
All you need to do is make up your mind,
To start living in your abundant life,
That you inherited through Christ,
All lack and debt will have to cease,
And all you will see is much increase,
So walk in who you were created to be,
And finally embrace your true identity,
Your dreams will become reality soon,
But only if you experience life in bloom.

United to Inspire Hope

"Generations of Hope" is this year's theme,
Embraced by our Law United Way campaign team,
An energetic campaign leader and 26 volunteers,
Joined together as a team to inspire our peers,
By helping you to connect to why we give,
To the Houston community where we live,
For the United Way touches one in every two,
And provides resources to help them through,
Meeting the needs of the full circle of life too,
Children, families, and seniors to name a few,
For those who just need a helping hand,
And a little encouragement to help them stand,
Many people are less fortunate than us,
So giving from our heart is truly a must,
It will take all of us in Law to reach our goal,
So it's important that we understand our role,
By putting our actions behind what we say,
And learning how to do it the "United Way,"
Just imagine the big impact that we can make,
Commitment and a little time is all it takes,
We know that everyone has to do their part,
Giving individual contributions is just a start,

We also need volunteers to help us give back,
To fill the void where our community lacks,
People need to know how much we care,
And see how much we are willing to share,
So remember to bring your gifts in kind,
And make sure you keep our events in mind,
Now is the time that we all get connected,
But not just because we know it's expected,
For there is no storm that we can't weather,
When we realize we do it better together,
Although all our efforts can't help everyone,
We can bring hope to generations to come,
Making a difference by helping people cope,
But only when we're "United to Inspire Hope."

REST STOP 4

"Find the journey's end in every stop."
—*Ralph Waldo Emerson*

When traveling to a global city like London, the best way to see the city is on a "hop on, hop off" sightseeing big bus tour, which allows you to get on and off at major landmarks. After you get a feel for the city, you can select the specific sites that you want to go back to visit. This is your chance to rest and refuel, so you can grab lunch, go to the restroom, buy souvenirs or decide what else you need for the rest of the trip.

After reading the poetic expressions about the process of discovering your real identity after a traumatic experience (like my near fatal car accident) and how hope can overflow in your life, you must hop off at this fourth rest stop to refuel and reflect on what you need during this part of the journey.

REFUEL:

Take a breath to rest your mind, nourish your soul and refresh your spirit by meditating on the following scriptures:

Genesis 1:27

Psalm 139:14

Romans 5:3-
2 Corinthians 5:17
1 Peter 2:9   87

REFLECT:

Reflect on your personal thoughts, feelings and observations from this part of the journey and write them down on the following "Reflect on the Journey" page.

REFLECT ON THE JOURNEY

RESUME THE JOURNEY

Let's get back on the bus! My last "hop on, hop off" big bus city tour was during my vacation in Montreal, Canada. My double decker bus included everything I needed to get to my destination—a city map with the tour stops, headphones to listen to the pre-recorded commentary, and tickets to my selected attractions. Make sure you have everything you need to get to where you're going before you hop back on the bus. Before we resume the journey, you should write down the lessons learned from your reflections below.

____

____

____

____

____

____

____

____

Chapter 5

Poetic Expressions on
Legacy and Purpose

My 20-Year Legal Legacy

My legal journey began over 20 years ago,
After passing the bar exam, I was ready to go,
I did not know what the future would hold,
But I was determined to reach my goals,
So let's take a stroll down memory lane,
As I tell my story about from where I came,
At the 14th Court of Appeals, I made my start,
Writing opinions for the judge was a big part,
Hearing oral arguments and reading briefs too,
The lessons I learned were more than I knew,
When my court assignment came to an end,
Another exciting phase of my journey began,
However, being in-house was not in my plans,
But only by divine intervention here I stand,
When I first walked through the company's door,
I was so eager to find out what was in store,
The Tort Litigation group was my first stop,
Depos, motions and jury trials became my lot,
After only a few months, I tried my first case,
And that's when I knew I was in the right place,
On to Commercial Litigation, I made a big switch,
Now handling bankruptcy cases without a glitch,

Then Legal Specialties – Environmental was next,
Trying to put the water regulations into context,
Environmental laws and regulations were all new,
It was well over six years before I was through,
Then Gas & Power Marketing Law was next on my list,
And this new commercial role came with a twist,
Giving advice and counsel to clients on natural gas,
Contracts and regulatory issues made the time pass fast,
Now it was time for me to get my Counsel wings,
As I continued to gain experience in new things,
In the meantime, I headed many committees too,
Pro Bono and Summer Associates to name a few,
My next move was way over to Chemical Law,
Which has been the most interesting area so far,
When I started out on the transactions side,
With complex divestments that I had to guide,
Then the commercial lawyer role, I began to play,
Drafting and negotiating contracts along the way,
While making time to give back to those in need,
Leading Law's United Way campaign to succeed,
By making a difference to help our community cope,
And embracing our theme, "United to Inspire Hope,"
When I think of this milestone, I could go on and on,
About all the memories that have come and gone,
That's why I am so grateful to have you join me,
As I joyfully celebrate my 20-year legal legacy.

A True Sisterhood

As we proudly celebrate one hundred and seven years,
Since Founder Ethel Hedgeman Lyle joined with her peers,
Deciding that our Greek-letter sorority would come first,
And that's when Alpha Kappa Alpha Sorority was birthed,
Our visionary founders were the ones to pave the way,
For the opportunities Black college women have today,
By promoting education and high standards too,
We've grown to over two hundred thousand from a few,
Graduate and undergraduate chapters everywhere,
Showing our community how much we really care,
Hearts that are loyal and hearts that are true,
For it's by merit and by culture that we strive to do,
We are much more than just those pretty girls,
Who wear pink and green with their twenty pearls,
We embrace our mission of service to all mankind,
And freely give of our talents, treasures and time,
We must carry forth the torch of our founders' legacy,
By all of us working together and promoting unity,
In the words of pioneer, Dr. King, "either we go up together,"
"Or we will go down together,"
We must pass on all the wisdom we've been told,
Since we know that nurturing the ivy is our goal,

For we are our sisters' keeper is what we've said,
So we must give from the heart, not just our head,
That's the reason why we love to help each other,
Because we already know there is no other,
Like our loving sorors that always have our back,
And are ready to stand in and take up the slack,
The great dreams of our founders will take place,
But only if we remain strong and finish our race,
For to whom much is given, much is required of us,
So our commitment and dedication is a must,
For now we need to have all hands on deck,
Because there's a lot we have not achieved yet,
So as we take this time to pay tribute to our past,
And launch new dimensions of service that will last,
Once we've given and sacrificed all that we could,
That's when we'll know we have a true sisterhood.

Family Ties

As we celebrate this Thanksgiving season,
I am grateful to God for so many reasons,
But I want to thank Him most for my family,
And how He put us together to fulfill destiny,
We can't pick our family like we do our friends,
Only God knows why He chose to make us kin,
Because we are not just by blood connected,
But by the years of memories we've collected,
And the ties to our matriarch's life and legacy,
Which will forever touch our lives into eternity,
Twelve years ago, we all suffered a great loss,
And now it's time for us to count up the cost,
It divided our family more than we know,
But it was an opportunity for us all to grow,
We don't know why things were so hard,
However, all we can do is just trust God,
Our family's name is destined to be great,
If we walk in our purpose before it's too late,
We already know our family roots run deep,
And whatever we sow is what we will reap,
So our family ties we must never lose sight,
And work together to make things right,

For if God is the center of our family tree,
A three-fold cord can't be broken easily,
So if we say we love God who we can't see,
We must be willing to forgive our own family,
We may not always agree with each other,
But we can love and respect one another,
For sticks and stones may break our bones,
But whoever said words never hurt was wrong,
We can't change the things that were said,
But we can deal in truth and move ahead,
For a house that is divided cannot stand,
So we must unite and walk hand in hand,
Then from our past we can finally be free,
If we just remember that "We Are Family,"
Blood is thicker than water is what they say,
So to stay connected, we have to pave the way,
For love is the tie that binds us all from the heart,
It's stronger than what's tried to tear us apart,
So we must refuse to believe the enemy's lies,
Because he can't break our strong family ties.

There Is No Place Like Home

The Lord led me to the house that He had in store for me,
And I could hardly believe what my eyes would see,
When I first saw a glimpse of this beautiful new place,
I was in awe and had a real big smile on my face,
Except the Lord builds the house, the work is in vain,
So I decided to claim my new home in Jesus' name,
My making that one move was the domino effect,
That shifted me into the many blessings God had next,
The Lord showed me my house in a dream long ago,
So all I had to do was follow His lead and get in the flow,
I've enjoyed traveling the world from Singapore to Rome,
But I can truly say, "there is no place like home."

A Warm New Home

Now I can finally settle in,
After celebrating with family and friends,
The blessing of my new home,
And everything that comes along,
Thank you for being a part,
Of warming my home and my heart!

A Heart of Gold

We're honored to give tribute to our dear mother,
She was truly one of a kind and like no other,
Her presence made the world a better place,
And she lit up a room with the smile on her face,
A genuine and beautiful person inside and out,
For her love and support, we could never doubt,
The most generous person that we'll ever know,
Not just with words, but her actions would show,
How much she loved her girls with all her heart,
And sacrificed all that she had from the start,
She protected us and made sure we had no lack,
And we knew that she always had our back,
She had wisdom and strength from God above,
And was not afraid to speak the truth in love,
Her faith made us believe that we could fly,
And gave us wings, so we could touch the sky,
Whenever we got weary and wanted to quit,
She told us boldly that we better handle it,
She taught us many life lessons and how to fight,
And showed us how to stand up for what's right,
She helped make all of our dreams come true,
And trusted that the Lord would see us through,

She had always pushed us to be our very best,
And refused to let us settle for anything less,
She set very high standards for us to achieve,
And told us it's more blessed to give than receive,
She overcame many obstacles along the way,
And her winning spirit is forever here to stay,
She lived life to the fullest without any regrets,
But the story of her life has not been told yet,
Her grandkids were her joy and inspiration,
And to our family she gave her full dedication,
For we are so blessed to carry on her legacy,
And will forever cherish her precious memories,
She'll be remembered for many things if the truth be told,
But most of all because she had "A Heart of Gold"!

♥ In Loving Memory of My Mother ♥
Dianne Gladney McBride
August 16, 1951 – October 22, 2017

We Need a Leader

Who is not afraid to speak up or fight,
And will stand up for our civil rights,
Who is committed to advance our cause,
And in hard times will not push pause,
Who will fight for justice and equality,
And understands the value of diversity,
Who embraces all of the hard work ahead,
And will follow through with what he said,
Who recognizes the needs of our community,
And will sacrifice to seize every opportunity,
Who will uplift those who are pushed down,
And teach them how to stand their ground,
Who will be able to see through all the smoke,
And knows why it is so important to #staywoke.

Rest Well, My Friend

When you first stopped by my mother's bookstore,
I saw your smiling face as you walked in the door,
The Lord divinely connected us and blessed me twice,
Not only with a true friend, but also a sister in Christ,
You were bold and knew how to fast, fight and pray,
And you always had my back all along the way,
A true woman of faith who stood on the Word,
And your servant heart could always be heard,
I will miss all the things that you say and do,
But most of all, I will just miss seeing you,
With much courage, you fought a good fight,
And finished your course with heaven in sight,
You boldly kept the faith until the very end,
Because you knew that with the Lord, you win,
I know that one day I will see you again,
But until then, rest well, my friend.

My 50ᵗʰ Birthday Celebration

Thanks for celebrating my 50th birthday,
It meant more to me than words can say,
I can't believe the time has passed so fast,
But I want you to know that I had a blast,
An amazing night with family and friends,
A red carpet event from beginning to end,
We had the golden awards and old school dancing too,
But it was so special just because of you,
So there's no need for me to think twice,
I am blessed to be living the GOLDEN life.

Happy Birthday to My Sister

I'm so excited to celebrate my sister's birthday,
She means more to me than words can say,
God made us sisters and love made us friends,
And I know she has my back until the end,
She is beautiful, charming, witty and smart,
And her sparkling personality will win your heart,
She's a true woman of God and anointed too,
Grand and over the top just to name a few,
She has touched my life in so many ways,
So I pray that many blessings will fill her day.

Waiting on a Dream Man

Who loves God and puts Him first,
And loves me as Christ loves the church,
Who is willing to fully commit to me,
And takes actions to make me happy,
Who wants to hear about how I feel,
And is not afraid to just keep it real,
Who wants to give me his full attention,
And can be honest about his intentions,
Who shows me how much I mean to him,
And does not just show up on a whim,
Who will cherish and protect my heart,
And does not do things to tear it apart,
Who accepts me for who I really am,
And knows how to get with the program,
Who will always be my best friend,
And my ride or die to the very end,
Who believes no storm we can't weather,
And knows that we do it better together,
Who wants others to know he's my man,
And takes steps so we walk hand in hand,
Who has plenty of time to spend with me,
And doesn't care how busy he may be,

Who understands that God is his source,
And treats me like a queen of course,
Who is the man that God called him to be,
And a priest, prophet and king for me,
Who truly walks by faith in all he does,
And he puts his full trust in God above,
Who is willing to fully let me into his life,
And know the favor I bring as his wife.

REST STOP 5

"A journey does not end when it ends."
—*Guy Gavriel Kay*

While traveling a short distance within most major cities, you can get where you're going faster and cheaper by taking an Uber rather than a taxi or rental car. If you need a ride, you can get on the Uber app, put in your destination, confirm the fee, track the vehicle and wait to get picked up. The ride is like a rest stop because you can sit back, relax and let someone else do the driving. Everything you need can be done on the app, including payment.

After reading the poetic expressions about how finding your purpose and living your legacy can be a defining moment in your life, you must stop at this fifth rest stop to refuel and reflect on what you need during this part of the journey.

REFUEL:

Take a breath to rest your mind, nourish your soul and refresh your spirit by meditating on the following scriptures:

Deuteronomy 30:19

John 10:10

2 Corinthians 5:8

Romans 14:8

Revelation 21:4

REFLECT:

Reflect on your personal thoughts, feelings and observations from this part of the journey and write them down on the following "Reflect on the Journey" page.

REFLECT ON THE JOURNEY

RESUME THE JOURNEY

My ride is here! When traveling for work or leisure, I usually take an Uber ride to and from the airport, so I don't have to worry about driving or parking. I already know the estimated time of arrival and cost to get to my destination. I get dropped off at the front door, so I can just sit back and relax until I get there.

All good things must come to an end. We have finally reached our destination on "My Journey," which is a place of faith. Similar to the Uber ride, I have learned how to let go and let God take the wheel in my life since He has already ordered my steps and stops. I trust him to get me safely to my purpose and destiny along my journey.

Thanks for being a part of my journey! I hope that your faith was renewed and you gained insight from my journey that you can apply to your own journey. Sometimes you need to let someone else (the Lord) who knows where you're going to do the driving, so you can enjoy the journey. Now it's time for you to resume your personal journey and decide how you plan to navigate your trip. Keep the faith and be encouraged!

About the Author

DeMonica D. Gladney, Esquire, is a native of Houston, Texas. She received her Bachelor of Science degree in Criminal Justice, *cum laude*, from Lamar University and Doctor of Jurisprudence, *cum laude*, from the University of Houston Law Center. She began her legal career as a Briefing Attorney for the Texas Fourteenth Court of Appeals in Houston, Texas and is now Senior Counsel for ExxonMobil.

DeMonica is a past President of the Houston Lawyers Association, Chair of the African-American Lawyers Section of the State Bar of Texas, and Chair of the National Bar Association's (NBA) Women Lawyers Division. She is also a member of the Houston Bar Association and the Corporate Counsel Women of Color. DeMonica has received many awards for her legal service, including the NBA Distinguished Scroll of Women Lawyers Award, the NBA Presidential Award and the Top 50 Black Attorneys in Houston—Super Attorney Award.

In addition to a successful legal career, DeMonica is an accomplished writer, poet and inspirational speaker. She is the bestselling author of *Identity Theft: Discovering the Real You*, *Willing to Wait: From Revelation to Manifestation*, and *Reflections from God*. She has received many awards for her literary work, including the i10-Media Influential Award for Authors and the Houston's Favorite Author Award. She has been featured on the Daystar Television Network and various television and radio talk shows around the country and in print media.

DeMonica is a proud member of the Mu Kappa Omega Chapter of Alpha Kappa Alpha Sorority, Inc. and a Silver Star honoree for her 25 years of service. She is a committed member of Covenant Glen Church and serves in the legal ministry.

Identity Theft is an inspiring, practical guide for those who desire to walk in their "true identity" by understanding God's purpose and destiny for their lives. The book will provide an eye-opening analysis on how to recognize when one's spiritual identity has been stolen and the keys to complete restoration and healing on the journey to discovering who you really are in Christ.

Willing to Wait is a practical and insightful survival guide for those who are frustrated or impatient about being in God's "waiting" room. While other books may talk about the need to wait, *Willing to Wait* goes even further and reveals in four key steps "how" to effectively wait on God's will and perfect timing.

Reflections from God is a powerful and innovative collection of poems arranged around major themes such as faith, life, love and mothers as reflected through the eyes of God. *Reflections from God* gives new meaning to the importance of having spiritual insight into the many changes and challenges that you face in everyday life.